ROCK RIFFS

CD INCLUDED

for Alto Saxophone

Alto Saxophone performed by
Jason Goldsmith

ISBN 978-1-4234-6212-5

HAL•LEONARD®
CORPORATION

7777 W. BLUEMOUND RD. P.O. BOX 13819 MILWAUKEE, WI 53213

Visit Hal Leonard Online at
www.halleonard.com

CONTENTS

PAGE	TITLE	CD TRACK
4	Ain't talkin' 'bout love - VAN HALEN	1
5	Another One Bites the Dust - QUEEN	2
4	Aqualung - JETHRO TULL	3
5	Back In Black - AC/DC	4
6	Barracuda - HEART	5
4	Carry On Wayward Son - KANSAS	6
7	Crazy Train - OZZY OSBOURNE	7
7	Day Tripper - THE BEATLES	8
7	Eye of the Tiger - SURVIVOR	9
8	Frankenstein - EDGAR WINTER GROUP	10
8	Godzilla - BLUE ÖYSTER CULT	11
6	I Feel Fine - THE BEATLES	12
8	Iron Man - BLACK SABBATH	13
9	The Joker - STEVE MILLER BAND	14
10	La Grange - ZZ TOP	15
10	Layla - DEREK AND THE DOMINOS	16
9	Message in a Bottle - THE POLICE	17
9	Money - PINK FLOYD	18
11	Oh, Pretty Woman - ROY ORBISON	19
11	Owner of a Lonely Heart - YES	20
11	Proud Mary - CREEDENCE CLEARWATER REVIVAL	21
12	Refugee - TOM PETTY & THE HEARTBREAKERS	22
12	Rock You Like a Hurricane - SCORPIONS	23
12	Smells Like Teen Spirit - NIRVANA	24
13	Smoke on the Water - DEEP PURPLE	25
13	Stayin' Alive - THE BEE GEES	26
13	Sunshine of Your Love - CREAM	27
14	Sweet Home Alabama - LYNYRD SKYNYRD	28
15	Walk This Way - AEROSMITH	29
14	You Really Got Me - THE KINKS	30
	TUNING NOTES	31

Ain't Talkin' 'Bout Love

Words and Music by David Lee Roth, Edward Van Halen, Alex Van Halen and Michael Anthony

Artist: Van Halen
Album: *Van Halen*
Year: 1978

Trivia: "Ain't Talkin' 'Bout Love" was one of the few David Lee Roth-era Van Halen songs that his successor Sammy Hagar was willing to perform live when he joined the band in the mid 1980s.

Aqualung

Music by Ian Anderson
Lyrics by Jennie Anderson

Artist: Jethro Tull
Album: *Aqualung*
Year: 1971

Trivia: Ian Anderson's then-wife Jennie took the photograph of a homeless person that influenced both the lyrics to this song and the *Aqualung* album cover.

Carry On Wayward Son

Words and Music by Kerry Livgren

Artist: Kansas
Album: *Leftoverture*
Year: 1976

Trivia: "Carry On Wayward Son" was a last-minute addition to the *Leftoverture* album. The album was written and ready to record, but the rest of the band didn't want to work on any additional material. Luckily they changed their minds as soon as they heard the song.

Another One Bites the Dust

Words and Music by John Deacon

Artist: Queen
Album: *The Game*
Year: 1980

Trivia: Though this was Queen's highest-charting single in the U.S., topping the Pop and even R&B charts, it appears on the list of songs compiled by Clear Channel Communications and its subsidiaries of songs that contain lyrics which may be unsuitable for airplay after the September 11, 2001 attacks.

Back in Black

Words and Music by Angus Young, Malcolm Young and Brian Johnson

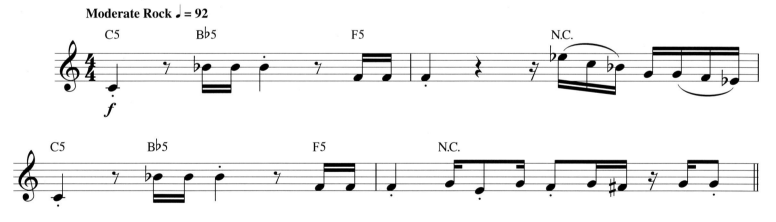

Artist: AC/DC
Album: *Back in Black*
Year: 1980

Trivia: This hit song from the album of the same title was the first to feature new singer Brian Johnson after the death of original front man, Bon Scott in 1980.

Barracuda

Words and Music by Nancy Wilson, Ann Wilson, Michael Derosier and Roger Fisher

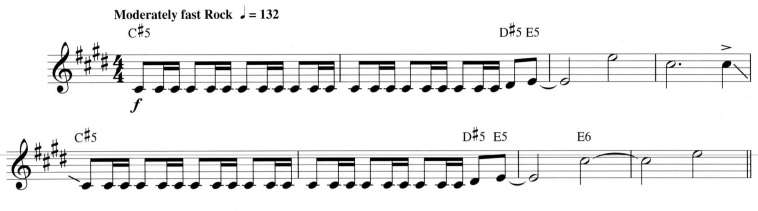

Artist: Heart
Album: *Little Queen*
Year: 1977

Trivia: The lyrics for this song were based on the negative (but not necessarily true) press the Wilson sisters received after the relationship with their first record label went sour.

I Feel Fine

Words and Music by John Lennon and Paul McCartney

* Chord symbols reflect implied tonality.

Artist: The Beatles
Album: *Beatles '65*
Year: 1964

Trivia: The original recording of this song was the very first to use guitar feedback.

Crazy Train
Words and Music by Ozzy Osbourne, Randy Rhoads and Bob Daisley

Artist: Ozzy Osbourne
Album: *Blizzard of Ozz*
Year: 1981

Trivia: The opening riff for "Crazy Train" is popular in professional sports, as it is the walk-up music for numerous baseball players and the introduction song for the New England Patriots football team.

Day Tripper
Words and Music by John Lennon and Paul McCartney

Artist: The Beatles
Album: *Yesterday…And Today*
Year: 1966

Trivia: Not only has "Day Tripper" been covered numerous times, but the riff to this #5 hit has been used by Devo and 2 Live Crew on their "The 4th Dimension" and "Fraternity Record" tracks, respectively.

Eye of the Tiger
Theme from ROCKY III
Words and Music by Frank Sullivan and Jim Peterik

Artist: Survivor
Album: *Eye of the Tiger*
Year: 1982

Trivia: Sylvester Stallone personally called Survivor's main songwriters, Frankie Sullivan and Jim Peterik, asking them to write the theme song to the *Rocky III* film after the record label's president played Stallone some tracks off the band's *Premonition* album. It was the #1 song of 1982.

Frankenstein
By Edgar Winter

Artist: Edgar Winter Group
Album: *They Only Come Out at Night*
Year: 1972

Trivia: Edgar Winter originally played drums on this song with brother Johnny Winter's trio. They called it "Double Drum Song" and it had no keyboards in it until the synthesizer made its way into the rock scene.

Godzilla
Words and Music by Donald Roeser

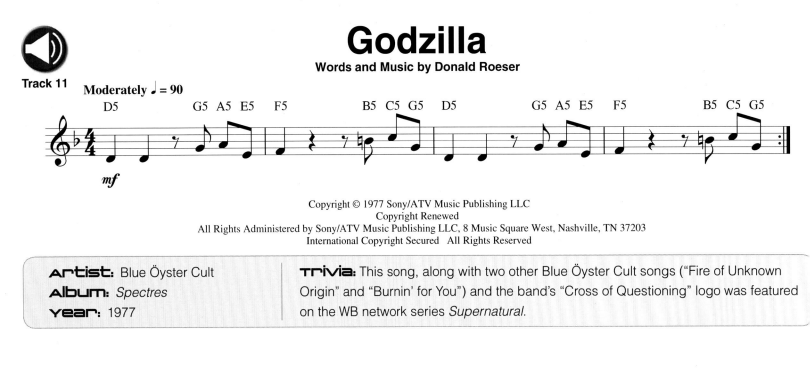

Artist: Blue Öyster Cult
Album: *Spectres*
Year: 1977

Trivia: This song, along with two other Blue Öyster Cult songs ("Fire of Unknown Origin" and "Burnin' for You") and the band's "Cross of Questioning" logo was featured on the WB network series *Supernatural*.

Iron Man
Words and Music by Frank Iommi, John Osbourne, William Ward and Terence Butler

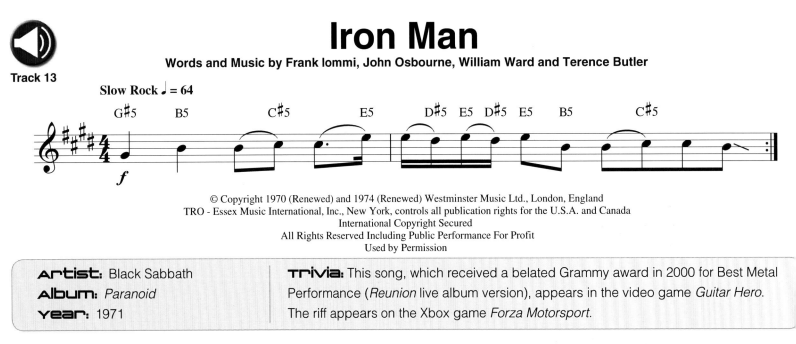

Artist: Black Sabbath
Album: *Paranoid*
Year: 1971

Trivia: This song, which received a belated Grammy award in 2000 for Best Metal Performance (*Reunion* live album version), appears in the video game *Guitar Hero*. The riff appears on the Xbox game *Forza Motorsport*.

The Joker

Words and Music by Steve Miller, Eddie Curtis and Ahmet Ertegun

Artist: Steve Miller Band
Album: *The Joker*
Year: 1973

Trivia: Some lyrics in this song refer to earlier Steve Miller songs ("Space Cowboy" and "Gangster of Love," for example), but there is a fair amount of controversy over the lyric "the pompatus of love." Miller claims he made the word up, however, a similar word (puppetutes) occurs in a 1954 Medallions song called "The Letter" ("discuss the puppetutes of love.") The word is also pondered in the 1996 film *The Pompatus of Love* starring Jon Cryer.

Track 17

Message in a Bottle

Music and Lyrics by Sting

Artist: The Police
Album: *Regatta de Blanc*
Year: 1979

Trivia: As Sting became more famous, his relationship with drummer Stewart Copeland began to deteriorate. However, both Copeland and guitarist Andy Summers were invited to Sting's wedding in 1992, where after much pressure from the guests they performed this song, along with their hit "Roxanne."

Money

Words and Music by Roger Waters

Track 18

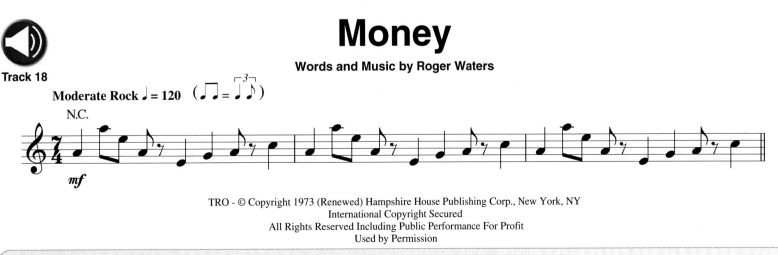

Artist: Pink Floyd
Album: *Dark Side of the Moon*
Year: 1976

Trivia: This song, written in Roger Waters's garden, is the only song in 7/4 time to hit the top 20 in the U.S.

La Grange

Words and Music by Billy F Gibbons, Dusty Hill and Frank Lee Beard

* Chord symbols reflect basic harmony.

Artist: ZZ Top
Album: *Tres Hombres*
Year: 1973

Trivia: This song is about the Texas Chicken Ranch: the brothel on which the film *The Best Little Whorehouse in Texas* is based.

Layla

Words and Music by Eric Clapton and Jim Gordon

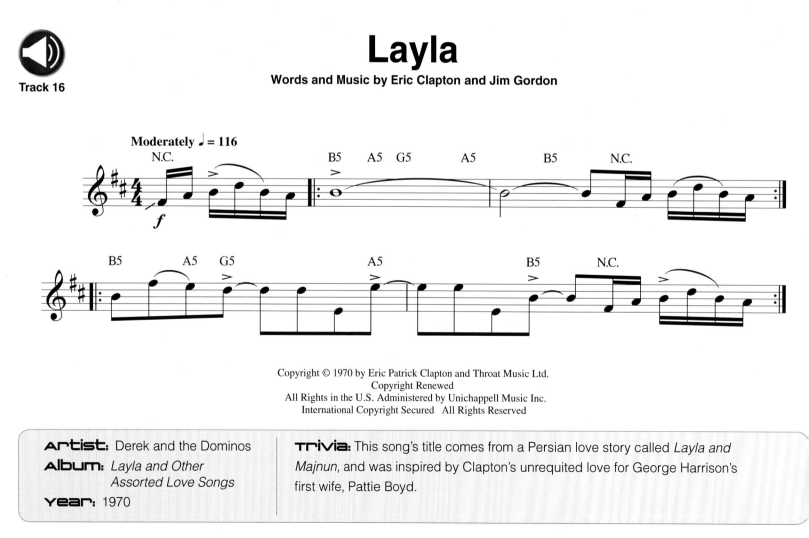

Artist: Derek and the Dominos
Album: *Layla and Other Assorted Love Songs*
Year: 1970

Trivia: This song's title comes from a Persian love story called *Layla and Majnun,* and was inspired by Clapton's unrequited love for George Harrison's first wife, Pattie Boyd.

Oh, Pretty Woman
Words and Music by Roy Orbison and Bill Dees

Artist: Roy Orbison
Album: *Orbisongs*
Year: 1965

Trivia: In 1989, controversial rap group 2 Live Crew sampled a portion of this song for a parody song called "Pretty Woman." The group's management requested a license from the song's publisher but was denied. However, 2 Live Crew recorded their parody anyway. The publisher sued for copyright infringement and unfair use, and the case was heard by the U.S. Supreme Court. The Court ruled in favor of 2 Live Crew, and stated that a for-profit parody may be protected under fair use law.

Owner of a Lonely Heart
Words and Music by Trevor Horn, Jon Anderson, Trevor Rabin and Chris Squire

Artist: Yes
Album: *90125*
Year: 1983

Trivia: This song was Yes' highest charting hit, reaching #1 in the U.S. The album *90125* introduced a new updated sound for this classic progressive rock band.

Proud Mary
Words and Music by John Fogerty

Artist: Creedence Clearwater Revival
Album: *Bayou Country*
Year: 1969

Trivia: Written on a steamboat called the "Mary Elizabeth," this song became the band's first top 10 hit on the U.S. Pop charts. Over the years, it has been covered by a wide variety of artists, including Elvis Presley and actor Leonard Nimoy.

Refugee
Words and Music by Tom Petty and Mike Campbell

Moderate Rock ♩ = 116

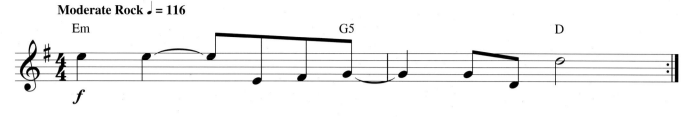

Artist: Tom Petty &
The Heartbreakers
Album: *Damn the Torpedoes*
Year: 1979

Trivia: Roughly six months before the release of "Refugee" as a single, Tom Petty had to file for bankruptcy. However, the *Damn the Torpedoes* album would prove to be his breakthrough hit.

Rock You Like a Hurricane
Words and Music by Herman Rarebell, Klaus Meine and Rudolf Schenker

Moderate Rock ♩ = 124

Artist: Scorpions
Album: *Love at First Sting*
Year: 1984

Trivia: It took twelve years for the Scorpions to break the U.S. top 40 chart, which they did thanks to this 1984 single.

Smells Like Teen Spirit
Words and Music by Kurt Cobain, Krist Novoselic and Dave Grohl

Driving Rock ♩ = 116

Artist: Nirvana
Album: *Nevermind*
Year: 1991

Trivia: Kurt Cobain got this song's unusual title when the phrase "Kurt Smells Like Teen Spirit" was spray painted on his wall by a friend. However, Kurt claimed he didn't know Teen Spirit was a deodorant brand name and regretted naming a commercial product in the song's title.

Smoke on the Water

Words and Music by Ritchie Blackmore, Ian Gillan, Roger Glover, Jon Lord and Ian Paice

Moderate Rock ♩ = 112

Artist: Deep Purple
Album: *Machine Head*
Year: 1972

Trivia: The lyrics to this song quite literally tell the story of an incident at the Montreaux Casino in Montreaux, Switzerland where a fire broke out at a Frank Zappa and the Mothers of Invention concert. Deep Purple had planned on recording the *Machine Head* album at the casino, but after the fire needed to scout out a new location, the first of which was a theater called The Pavilion. However, "Smoke on the Water" was the only song recorded at the theater because the neighbors complained about the noise.

Stayin' Alive

from the Motion Picture SATURDAY NIGHT FEVER

Words and Music by Barry Gibb, Robin Gibb and Maurice Gibb

Moderately ♩ = 104

Artist: The Bee Gees
Album: *Saturday Night Fever*
Year: 1977

Trivia: Besides the hugely successful *Saturday Night Fever* film, this song appears on the soundtracks for *Neighbors, Airplane!, Staying Alive* (the sequel to *Saturday Night Fever*), *Cadillac Man, Honey, I Blew Up the Kid, Bushwacked, Grumpier Old Men*, and *A Night at the Roxbury*. However, only the *Saturday Night Fever* soundtrack can boast that it is the best-selling soundtrack of all time in worldwide sales.

Sunshine of Your Love

Words and Music by Jack Bruce, Pete Brown and Eric Clapton

Moderately ♩ = 110

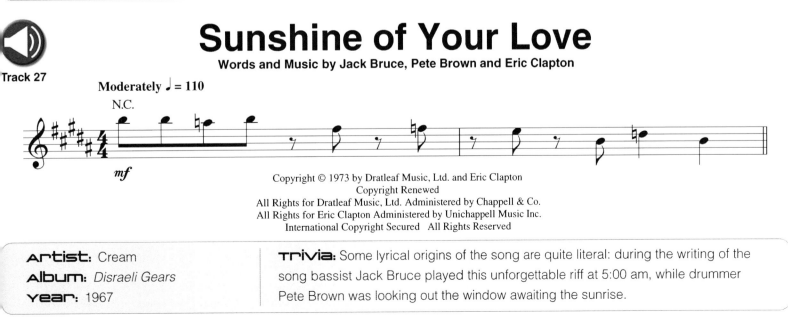

Artist: Cream
Album: *Disraeli Gears*
Year: 1967

Trivia: Some lyrical origins of the song are quite literal: during the writing of the song bassist Jack Bruce played this unforgettable riff at 5:00 am, while drummer Pete Brown was looking out the window awaiting the sunrise.

Sweet Home Alabama

Words and Music by Ronnie Van Zant, Ed King and Gary Rossington

Artist: Lynyrd Skynrd
Album: *Second Helping*
Year: 1974

Trivia: The many films in which this song has been featured include *8 Mile, Forrest Gump*, the remake of *The Texas Chainsaw Massacre*, and of course the 2002 movie of the same name (where pop singer Jewel performed it for the soundtrack). It is also the opening theme music for the NASCAR series of video games, and is played at least once during the broadcasts of NASCAR's Nextel Cup races in Talladega, Alabama.

You Really Got Me

Words and Music by Ray Davies

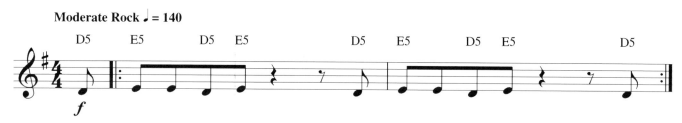

Artist: The Kinks
Album: *You Really Got Me*
Year: 1964

Trivia: The Kinks' record company almost didn't allow the recording of this #7 hit, whose groundbreaking guitar tone was achieved by Dave Davies slicing the surface of the speaker cone in his amplifier with a razor blade.

Walk This Way

Words and Music by Steven Tyler and Joe Perry

Moderate Rock ♩ = 112

Artist: Aerosmith
Album: *Toys in the Attic*
Year: 1975

Trivia: The title of this #10 (1976) and #4 (1986) hit was inspired by a line spoken by the character Igor in the 1974 film *Young Frankenstein.*

HAL•LEONARD INSTRUMENTAL PLAY-ALONG

WITH THESE FANTASTIC BOOK/CD PACKS, INSTRUMENTALISTS CAN PLAY ALONG WITH THEIR FAVORITE SONGS!

BROADWAY'S BEST

15 Broadway favorites arranged for the instrumentalist, including: Always Look on the Bright Side of Life • Any Dream Will Do • Castle on a Cloud • I Whistle a Happy Tune • My Favorite Things • Where Is Love? • and more.
00841974 Flute $10.95
00841975 Clarinet..................$10.95
00841976 Alto Sax.................$10.95
00841977 Tenor Sax..............$10.95
00841978 Trumpet.................$10.95
00841979 Horn......................$10.95
00841980 Trombone..............$10.95
00841981 Violin $10.95
00841982 Viola $10.95
00841983 Cello $10.95

CHRISTMAS CAROLS

15 favorites from the holidays, including: Deck the Hall • The First Noel • Good King Wenceslas • Hark! the Herald Angels Sing • It Came upon the Midnight Clear • O Christmas Tree • We Three Kings of Orient Are • and more.
00842132 Flute $10.95
00842133 Clarinet..................$10.95
00842134 Alto Sax.................$10.95
00842135 Tenor Sax..............$10.95
00842136 Trumpet.................$10.95
00842137 Horn......................$10.95
00842138 Trombone..............$10.95
00842139 Violin $10.95
00842140 Viola $10.95
00842141 Cello $10.95

CHRISTMAS FAVORITES

Includes 15 holiday favorites with a play-along CD: Blue Christmas • Caroling, Caroling • The Christmas Song (Chestnuts Roasting on an Open Fire) • Christmas Time Is Here • Do You Hear What I Hear • Here Comes Santa Claus (Right Down Santa Claus Lane) • (There's No Place Like) Home for the Holidays • I Saw Mommy Kissing Santa Claus • Little Saint Nick • Merry Christmas, Darling • O Bambino • Rudolph the Red-Nosed Reindeer • Santa Claus Is Comin' to Town • Snowfall
00841964 Flute $12.95
00841965 Clarinet..................$12.95
00841966 Alto Sax.................$12.95
00841967 Tenor Sax..............$12.95
00841968 Trumpet.................$12.95
00841969 Horn......................$12.95
00841970 Trombone..............$12.95
00841971 Violin $12.95
00841972 Viola $12.95
00841973 Cello $12.95

CLASSICAL FAVORITES

15 classic solos for all instrumentalists. Includes: Ave Maria (Schubert) • Blue Danube Waltz (Strauss, Jr.) • Für Elise (Beethoven) • Largo (Handel) • Minuet in G (Bach) • Ode to Joy (Beethoven) • Symphony No. 9 in E Minor ("From the New World"), Second Movement Excerpt (Dvorak) • and more.
00841954 Flute $10.95
00841955 Clarinet..................$10.95
00841956 Alto Sax.................$10.95
00841957 Tenor Sax..............$10.95
00841958 Trumpet.................$10.95
00841959 Horn......................$10.95
00841960 Trombone..............$10.95
00841961 Violin $10.95
00841962 Viola $10.95
00841963 Cello $10.95

CONTEMPORARY HITS

Play 15 of your pop favorites along with this great folio and full accompaniment CD. Songs include: Accidentally in Love • Calling All Angels • Don't Tell Me • Everything • Fallen • The First Cut Is the Deepest • Here Without You • Hey Ya! • If I Ain't Got You • It's My Life • 100 Years • Take My Breath Away (Love Theme) • This Love • White Flag • You Raise Me Up.
00841924 Flute $12.95
00841925 Clarinet..................$12.95
00841926 Alto Sax.................$12.95
00841927 Tenor Sax..............$12.95
00841928 Trumpet.................$12.95
00841929 Horn......................$10.95
00841931 Violin $12.95
00841932 Viola $12.95
00841933 Cello $12.95

DISNEY GREATS

Another great play-along collection of 15 Disney favorites, including: Arabian Nights • A Change in Me • Hawaiian Roller Coaster Ride • I'm Still Here (Jim's Theme) • It's a Small World • Look Through My Eyes • Supercalifragilisticexpialidocious • Where the Dream Takes You • Yo Ho (A Pirate's Life for Me) • and more.
00841934 Flute $12.95
00842078 Oboe.....................$12.95
00841935 Clarinet..................$12.95
00841936 Alto Sax.................$12.95
00841937 Tenor Sax..............$12.95
00841938 Trumpet.................$12.95
00841939 Horn......................$12.95
00841940 Trombone..............$12.95
00841941 Violin $12.95
00841942 Viola $12.95
00841943 Cello $12.95

ESSENTIAL ROCK

Instrumentalists will love jamming with a play-along CD for 15 top rock classics, including: Aqualung • Brown Eyed Girl • Crocodile Rock • Don't Stop • Free Bird • I Want You to Want Me • La Grange • Low Rider • Maggie May • Walk This Way • and more.
00841944 Flute $10.95
00841945 Clarinet..................$10.95
00841946 Alto Sax.................$10.95
00841947 Tenor Sax..............$10.95
00841948 Trumpet.................$10.95
00841949 Horn......................$10.95
00841950 Trombone..............$10.95
00841951 Violin $10.95
00841952 Viola $10.95
00841953 Cello $10.95

HIGH SCHOOL MUSICAL

Solo arrangements with CD accompaniment for 9 hits from the wildly popular Disney Channel original movie. Songs include: Bop to the Top • Breaking Free • Get'cha Head in the Game • I Can't Take My Eyes Off of You • Start of Something New • Stick to the Status Quo • We're All in This Together • What I've Been Looking For • When There Was Me and You.
00842121 Flute $12.95
00842122 Clarinet..................$12.95
00842123 Alto Sax.................$12.95
00842124 Tenor Sax..............$12.95
00842125 Trumpet.................$12.95
00842126 Horn......................$12.95
00842127 Trombone..............$12.95
00842128 Violin $12.95
00842129 Viola $12.95
00842130 Cello $12.95

ANDREW LLOYD WEBBER CLASSICS

12 solos from Webber's greatest shows complete with full band accompaniment on CD. Titles include: As If We Never Said Goodbye • Close Every Door • Don't Cry for Me Argentina • Everything's Alright • Go Go Go Joseph • Gus: The Theatre Cat • Love Changes Everything • The Music of the Night • Our Kind of Love • The Phantom of the Opera • Unexpected Song • Whistle Down the Wind.
00841824 Flute $14.95
00841825 Oboe.....................$14.95
00841826 Clarinet..................$14.95
00841827 Alto Sax.................$14.95
00841828 Tenor Sax..............$14.95
00841829 Trumpet.................$14.95
00841830 Horn......................$14.95
00841831 Trombone..............$14.95
00841832 Mallet Percussion ..$14.95
00841833 Violin $14.95
00841834 Viola $14.95
00841835 Cello $14.95

MOVIE MUSIC

15 hits from popular movie blockbusters of today, including: And All That Jazz • Come What May • I Am a Man of Constant Sorrow • I Believe I Can Fly • I Walk the Line • Seasons of Love • Theme from Spider Man • and more
00842089 Flute $10.95
00842090 Clarinet..................$10.95
00842091 Alto Sax.................$10.95
00842092 Tenor Sax..............$10.95
00842093 Trumpet.................$10.95
00842094 Horn......................$10.95
00842095 Trombone..............$10.95
00842096 Violin $10.95
00842097 Viola $10.95
00842098 Cello $10.95

TV FAVORITES

15 TV tunes arranged for instrumentalists, including: The Addams Family Theme • The Brady Bunch • Green Acres Theme • Happy Days • Johnny's Theme • Linus and Lucy • NFL on Fox Theme • Theme from The Simpsons • and more.
00842079 Flute $10.95
00842080 Clarinet..................$10.95
00842081 Alto Sax.................$10.95
00842082 Tenor Sax..............$10.95
00842083 Trumpet.................$10.95
00842084 Horn......................$10.95
00842085 Trombone..............$10.95
00842086 Violin $10.95
00842087 Viola $10.95
00842088 Cello $10.95

FOR MORE INFORMATION, SEE YOUR LOCAL MUSIC DEALER, OR WRITE TO:

HAL•LEONARD® CORPORATION

7777 W. BLUEMOUND RD. P.O. BOX 13819 MILWAUKEE, WI 53213

PRICES, CONTENTS AND AVAILABILITY ARE SUBJECT TO CHANGE WITHOUT NOTICE.

SOME PRODUCTS MAY NOT BE AVAILABLE OUTSIDE THE U.S.A.

DISNEY CHARACTERS AND ARTWORK © DISNEY ENTERPRISES, INC.

VISIT HAL LEONARD ONLINE AT
WWW.HALLEONARD.COM

0609